Vocabulary Sticker Books

At Home

W0082133

To Parents: Use the check boxes to note what words your child would be able to learn and say by themselves. You can also use this chart to track your child's progress. Check off each word your child learns as he or she completes this workbook.

Table of Contents

1 Home

To parents

Please remove the first sheet of stickers and give it to your child. This sheet of stickers is for exercises 1 through 3.

Paste the sticker onto each blank space while saying the object aloud. Then, find the objects along the bottom in the main picture and say them aloud.

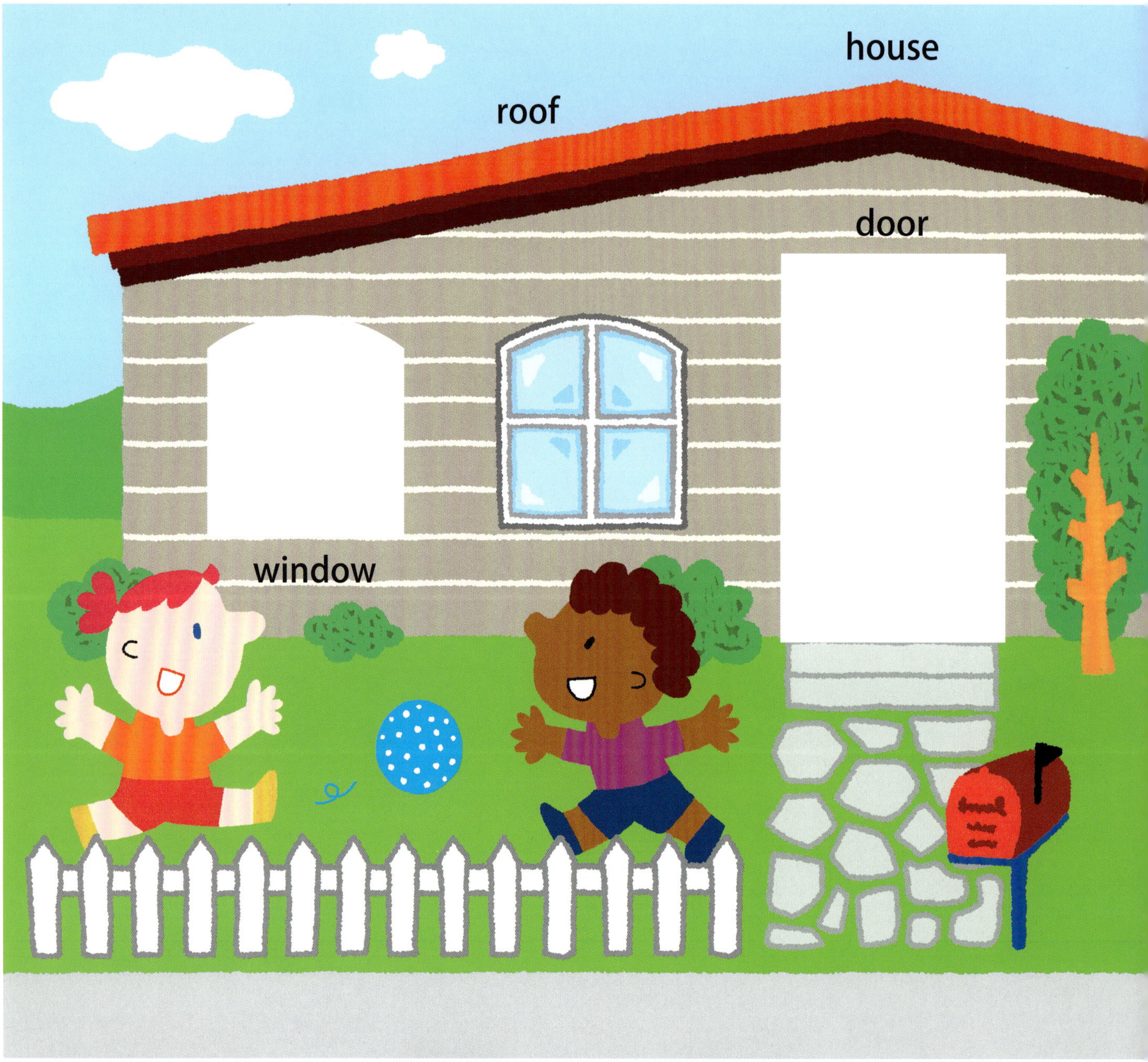

house

roof

door

window

house

door

window

roof

Done!

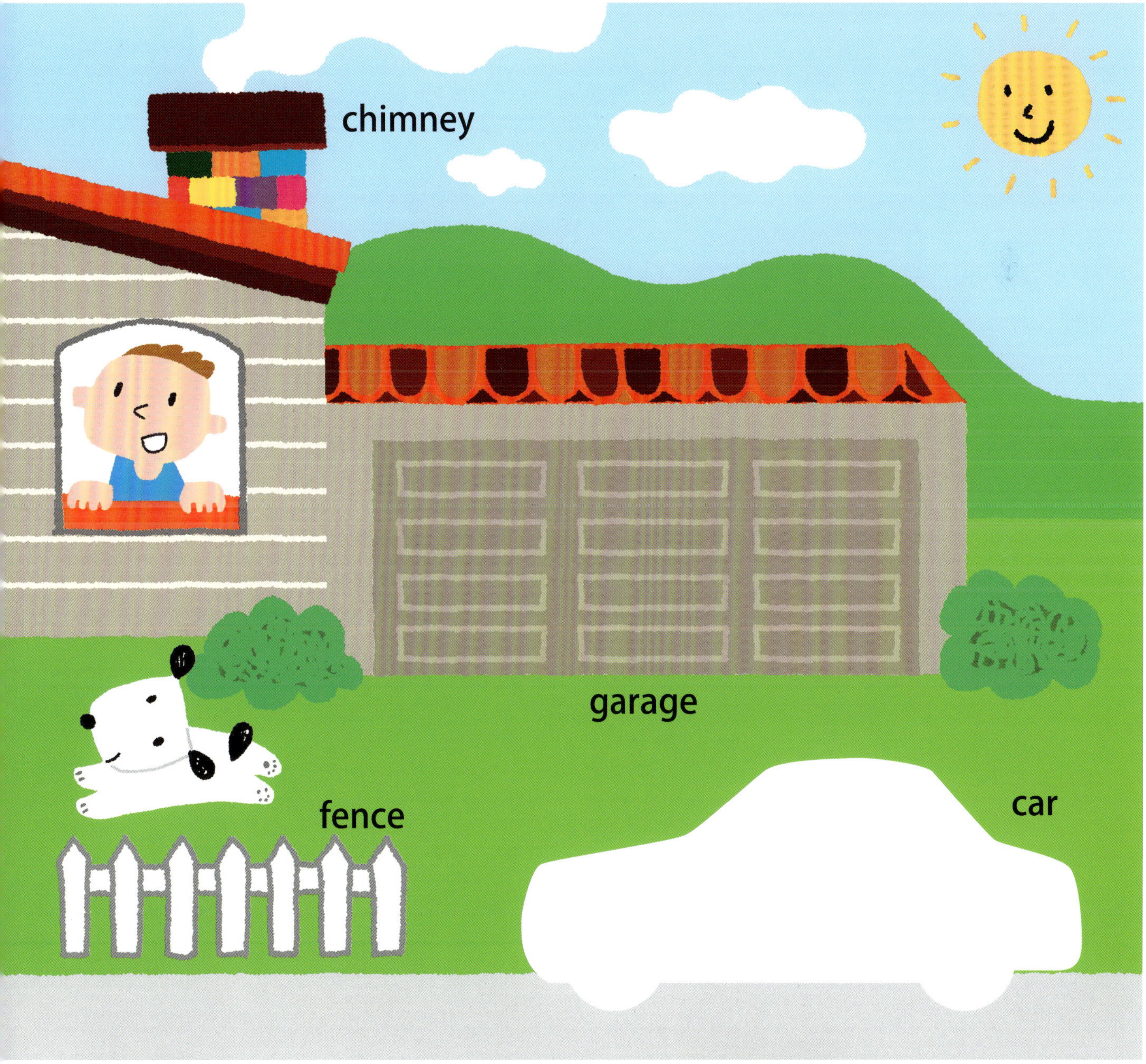

chimney

garage

fence

car

chimney

car

garage

fence

2 Family

To parents

People sometimes go by different names, like mother and father, or mom and dad. Even if your child uses a name different from the word in the illustration, offer a lot of praise. It would be nice to talk with your child about different names during or after this exercise.

Paste the sticker onto each blank space while saying the object aloud. Then, find the objects along the bottom in the main picture and say them aloud.

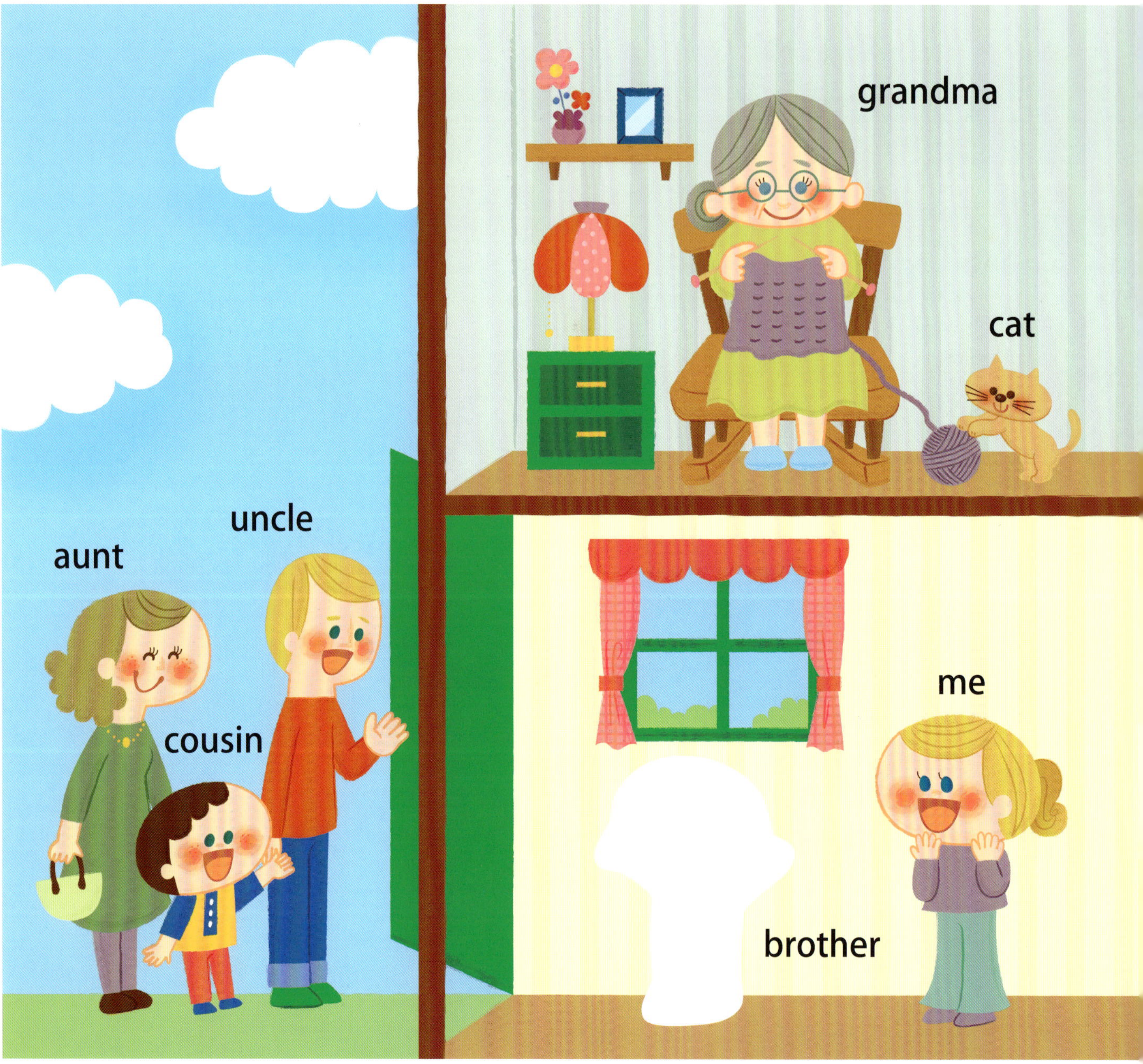
grandma
cat
uncle
aunt
cousin
me
brother

aunt
cousin
uncle
brother
me
grandma
cat

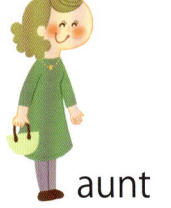

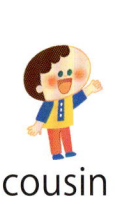

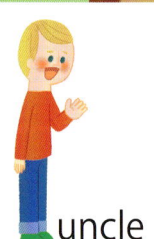

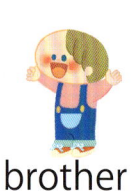

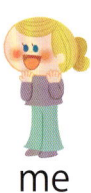

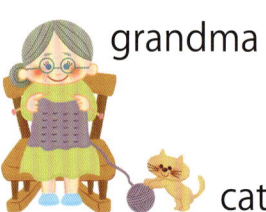

Done!

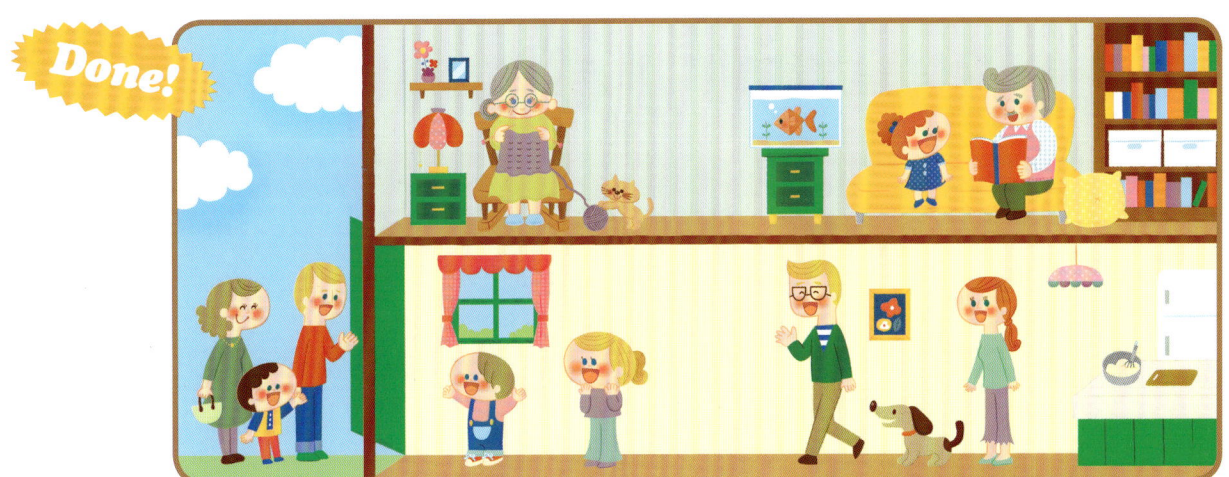

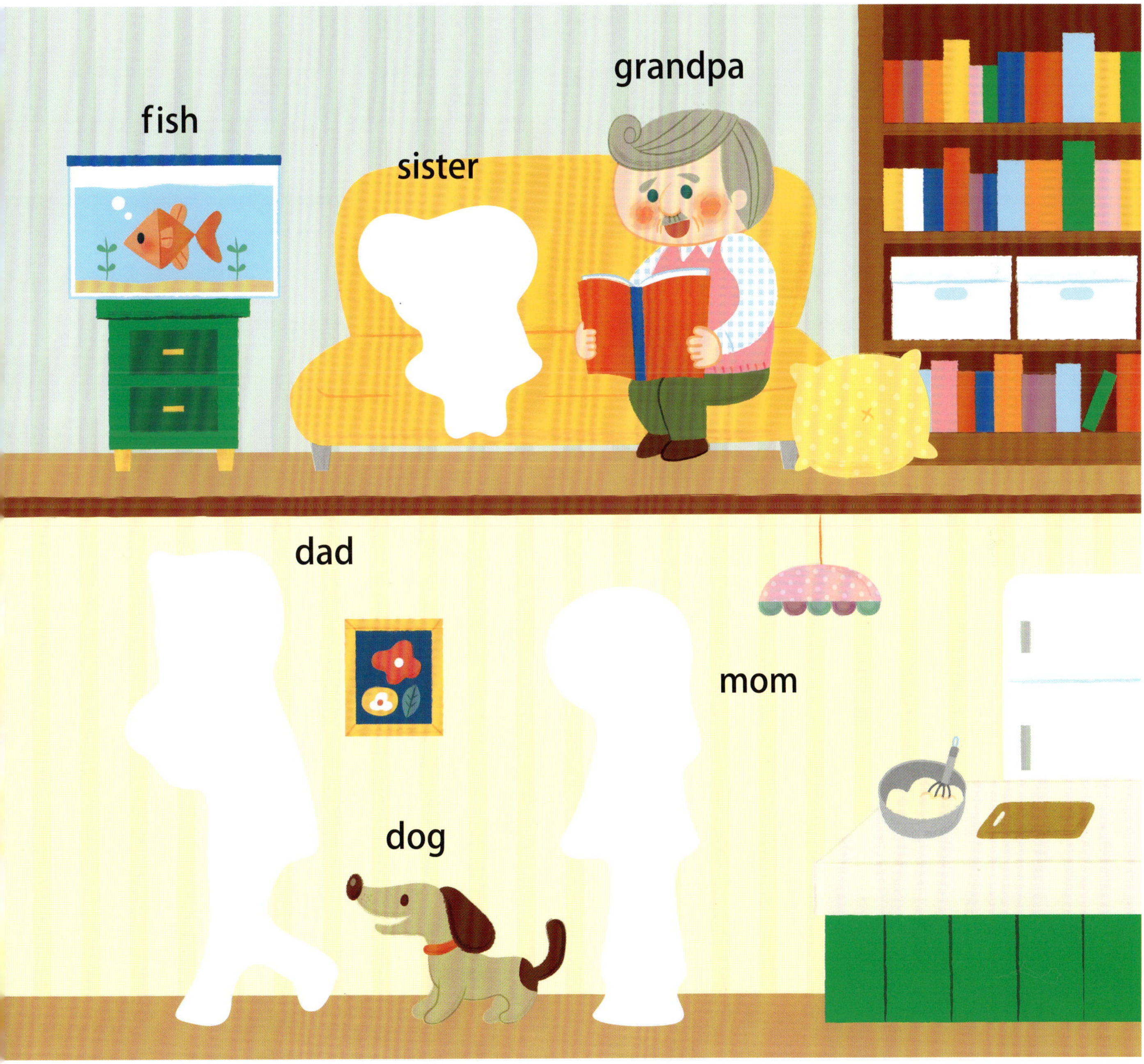
grandpa
fish
sister
dad
mom
dog

fish
sister
grandpa
dad
dog
mom

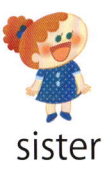

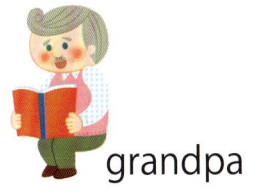

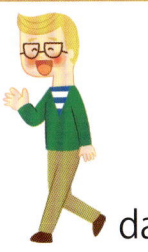

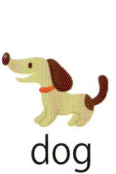

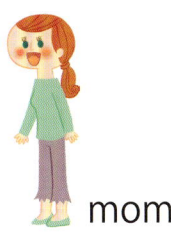

3 Living room

To parents

In the main picture, help your child look for the items along the bottom of the page. Finding the same picture twice will help increase your child's understanding of each object. Let him or her become familiar with the names of objects while having fun.

Paste the sticker onto each blank space while saying the object aloud. Then, find the objects along the bottom in the main picture and say them aloud.

piano

clock

TV

lamp

end table

TV remote

piano

clock

TV

rug

TV remote

lamp

Done!

painting

stairs

cushion

couch

armchair

rug

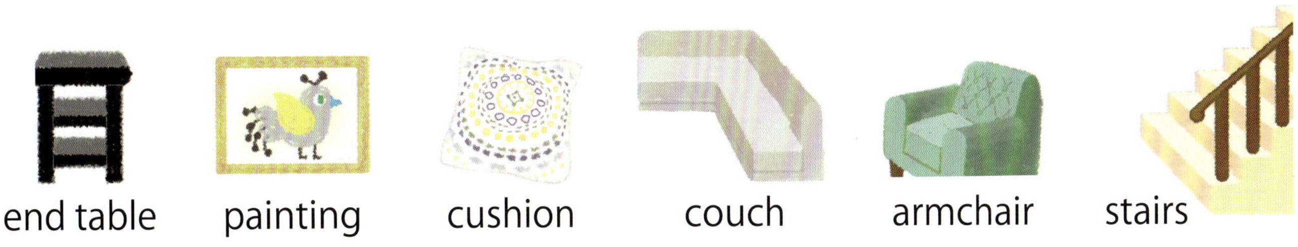

end table

painting

cushion

couch

armchair

stairs

4 Bathroom

To parents

If your child peels off the sticker in a hurry, it could rip. Please assist him or her by saying something cautious like, "Please peel the sticker off slowly." It is important you let your child practice peeling off and placing the stickers to help his or her fine motor development.

Paste the sticker onto each blank space while saying the object aloud. Then, find the objects along the bottom in the main picture and say them aloud.

washcloth

shower

bathtub

basket

soap

| washcloth | soap | shower | bathtub | basket | faucet |

mirror

laundry soap

faucet

washing machine

toilet

hamper

hair dryer

mirror

laundry soap

hamper

washing machine

hair dryer

toilet

5 Kitchen

Paste the sticker onto each blank space while saying the object aloud. Then, find the objects along the bottom in the main picture and say them aloud.

microwave

oven

refrigerator

dish

teapot

pot

refrigerator   microwave   oven   teapot   pot   dish

Done!

pan

blender

stove

toaster

dish towels

dish washer

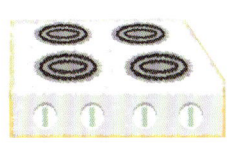

stove   pan   blender   toaster   dish towels   dish washer

6 Dining room

To parents

It is a good idea to say the words while pointing to new objects such as "glass." Children will become familiar with the new word while looking at the picture of the object. It is not necessary for them to memorize letters at this time.

Paste the sticker onto each blank space while saying the object aloud. Then, find the objects along the bottom in the main picture and say them aloud.

table

cup

bowl

cream

candlestick

tablecloth

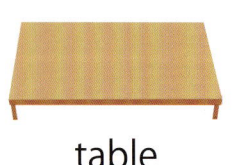

table

tablecloth

bowl

cream

cup

candlestick

Done!

plate

pitcher

water

glass

curtain

chair

 plate

 water

 pitcher

 glass

 chair

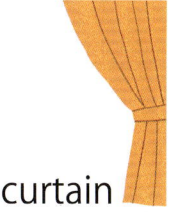 curtain

7 Breakfast

To parents

In sections 7 through 9, your child will learn various names of foods and cooking tools. You may use this activity to ask your child, "Do you have any favorite foods?" Say the name of the food or imitate eating it with your child.

Paste the sticker onto each blank space while saying the object aloud. Then, find the objects along the bottom in the main picture and say them aloud.

juice

toast

butter

spoon

cereal

orange

milk

butter

toast

orange

juice

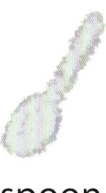

spoon

cereal

Done!

tea

jam

pancakes

apple

bananas

milk

jam

tea

pancakes

apple

bananas

8 Lunch

To parents

It is okay if your child places the sticker outside of the area at first. What is most important is that your child enjoys stickering.

Paste the sticker onto each blank space while saying the object aloud. Then, find the objects along the bottom in the main picture and say them aloud.

soup

knife

sandwich

fork

cheese

chips

cheese

soup

knife

fork

sandwich

chips

Done!

cookies

napkin

bread

jelly

salad

peanut butter

 cookies

 salad

 bread

 napkin

 jelly

 peanut butter

To parents

It would be nice to talk with your child about the food in this activity. You can ask, "Do you have any favorite dishes?" "What is your favorite food?"

Paste the sticker onto each blank space while saying the object aloud. Then, find the objects along the bottom in the main picture and say them aloud.

broccoli

chicken

green beans

pasta

carrots

potatoes

hamburger

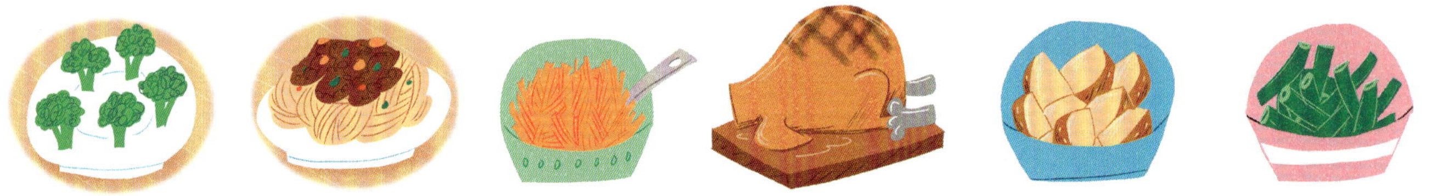

broccoli   pasta   carrots   chicken   potatoes   green beans

Done!

ham

meatballs

steak

pepper salt

hamburger   steak   ham   meatballs   pepper   salt

10 Front yard

To parents

In sections 10 through 12, there is a path in the picture for your child to trace with his or her finger. It may be a good idea to say the name of objects along the path such as flag, mailbox, or newspaper as your child traces the path.

Paste the sticker onto each blank space while saying the object aloud. Then, find the objects along the bottom in the main picture and say them aloud.

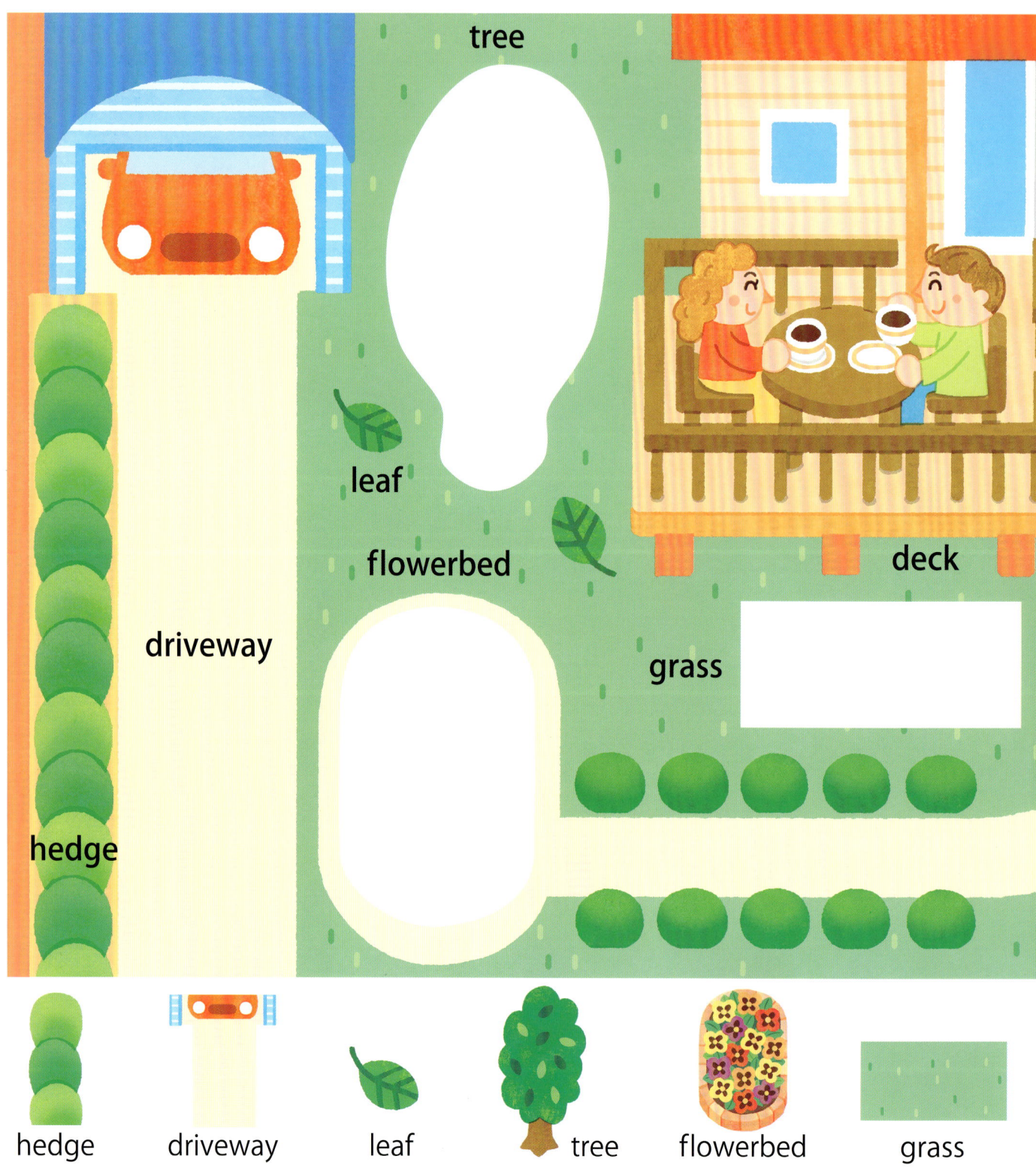

tree

leaf

flowerbed

deck

driveway

grass

hedge

| hedge | driveway | leaf | tree | flowerbed | grass |

Done!

flag

steps

path

mailbox

newspaper

deck

path

newspaper

steps

flag

mailbox

11 Back yard

To parents

It may be good to have your child say the name of each object on the path while tracing. Your child will learn new words such as slide, caterpillar, and rake in this way.

Paste the sticker onto each blank space while saying the object aloud. Then, find the objects along the bottom in the main picture and say them aloud.

flowers

lawn mower

shovel

seeds

watering can

ladybug

flowers

ladybug

shovel

watering can

lawn mower

seeds

swing

slide

bird

birdbath

caterpillar

rake

swing

slide

bird

birdbath

rake

caterpillar

Cleaning

To parents

In this picture, your child can pretend he or she is cleaning the dust path while tracing it with his or her finger. Have your child say the cleaning objects aloud as he or she plays.

Paste the sticker onto each blank space while saying the object aloud. Then, find the objects along the bottom in the main picture and say them aloud.

iron

vacuum

ironing board

broom

sponge

bucket

broom   iron   ironing board   sponge   vacuum   bucket

mop

water

deck brush

feather duster

dustpan

garbage can

feather duster   mop   water   deck brush   dustpan   garbage can

13 Bedroom

To parents

In sections 13 through 15, there are toys and clothes familiar to children. It could be fun if you compete with your child for a quick search of the objects along the bottom of the pages to see who can find them fastest in the main picture.

Paste the sticker onto each blank space while saying the object aloud. Then, find the objects along the bottom in the main picture and say them aloud.

dresser

pillow

bed

sheets

blanket

slippers

| dresser | bed | sheets | blanket | pillow | slippers |

teddy bear

night-light

night table

closet

pajamas

toy box

teddy bear

night-light

night table

toy box

pajamas

closet

14 Toys and school things

To parents

Peeling off and pasting tiny stickers is not an easy skill for young children to learn. Your child must gain the ability to control the fine movements of his or her fingers. When your child is finished with the activity, please offer a lot of praise.

Paste the sticker onto each blank space while saying the object aloud. Then, find the objects along the bottom in the main picture and say them aloud.

book

dollhouse

ball

board game

blocks

doll

doll   dollhouse   ball   board game   book   blocks

Done!

desk

pencil

notebook

backpack

truck

boat

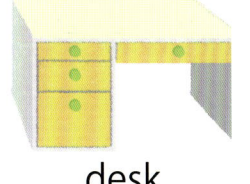 desk 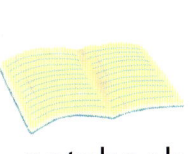 notebook  pencil  backpack  truck  boat

15 Clothes

To parents

This is the last page of this workbook. Has your child enjoyed stickering and learning new words? Use the award certificate at the back of the book to praise your child's best efforts.

Paste a clothing sticker freely onto each child while saying the object aloud. Then, find the objects along the bottom in the main picture and say them aloud.

jacket

socks

jacket   socks   cap   shirt   shorts   shoes

dress

jeans

     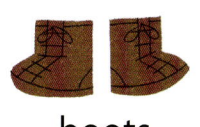

dress   hat   jeans   sweater   pants   boots

Certificate of Achievement

is hereby congratulated on completing

**Vocabulary Sticker Books
At Home**

Presented on _____ , 20 _____

_____

Parent or Guardian

KUMON

Stickers-1

To be used in 1

car

window

door

To be used in 2

brother

sister

dad

mom

To be used in 3

cushion

clock

TV

stairs

Stickers-2

To be used in 4

soap

washing machine

basket

mirror

To be used in 5

teapot

pot

microwave

toaster

To be used in 6

glass

cup

water

chair

Stickers-3

To be used in 7

apple

pancakes

milk

orange

To be used in 8

sandwich

cookies

soup

bread

steak

chicken

pasta

hamburger

To be used in 9

Stickers-4

To be used in 10

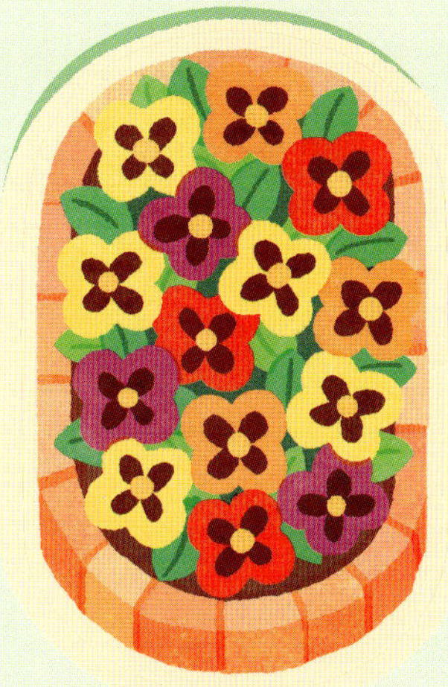

flower bed

tree

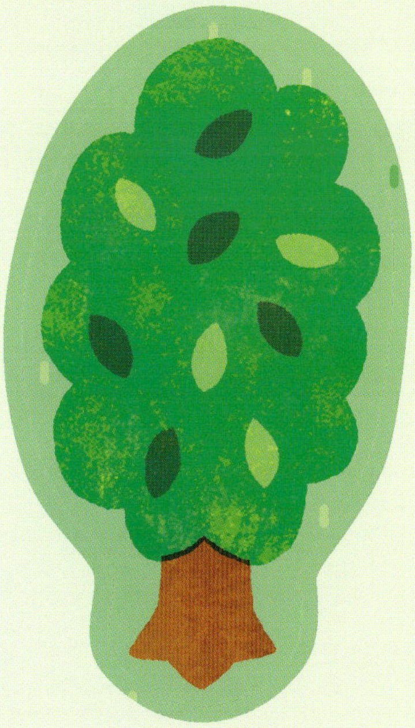

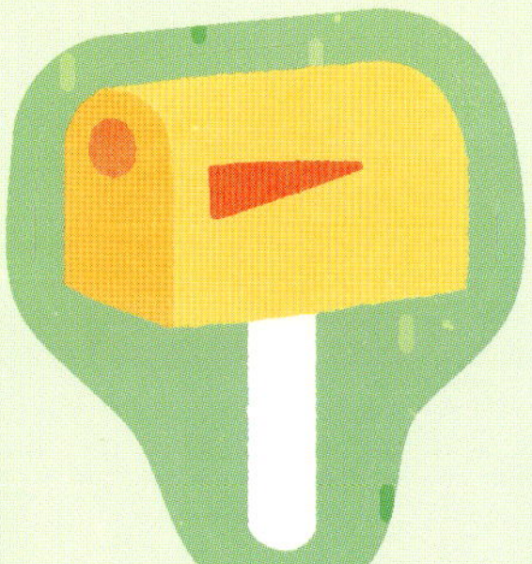

mailbox

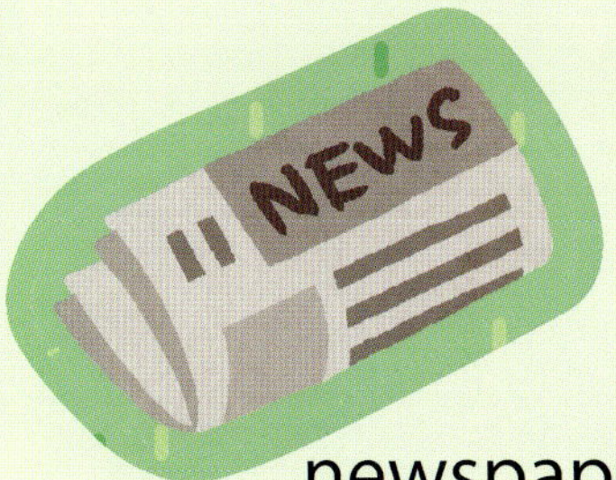

newspaper

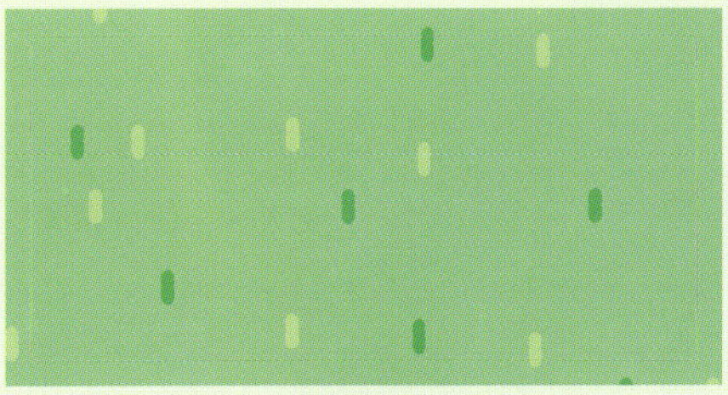

grass

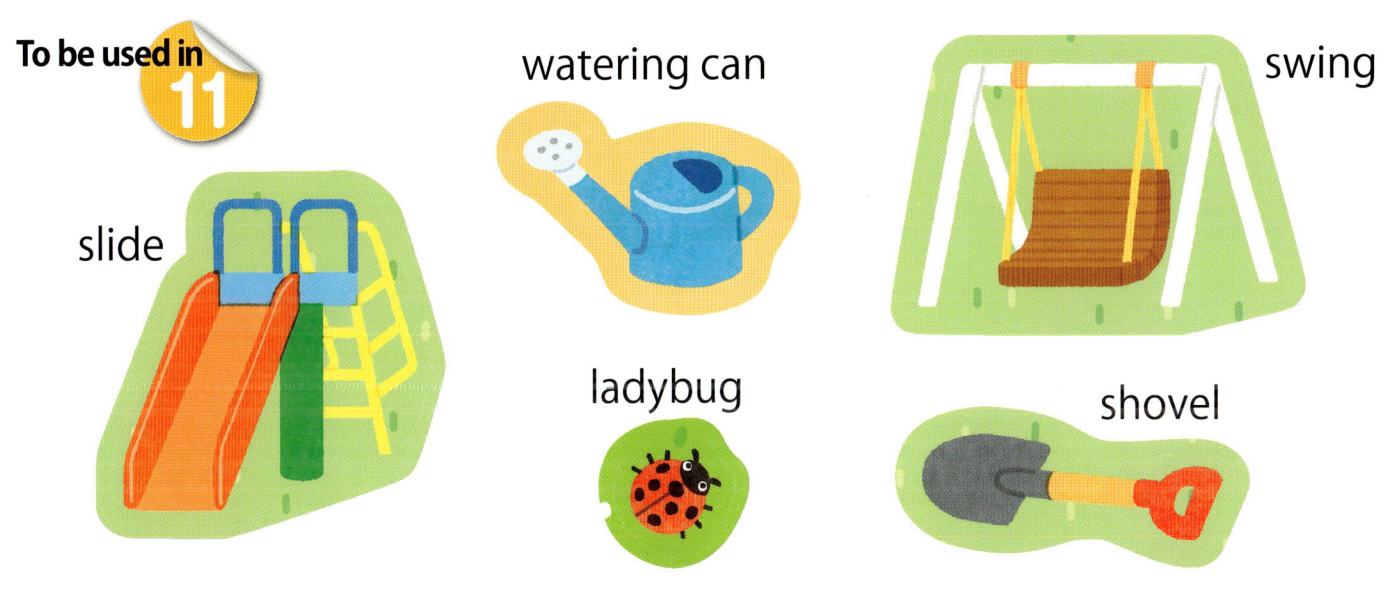

To be used in 11

watering can

swing

slide

ladybug

shovel

To be used in 12

dustpan

mop

iron

bucket

garbage can

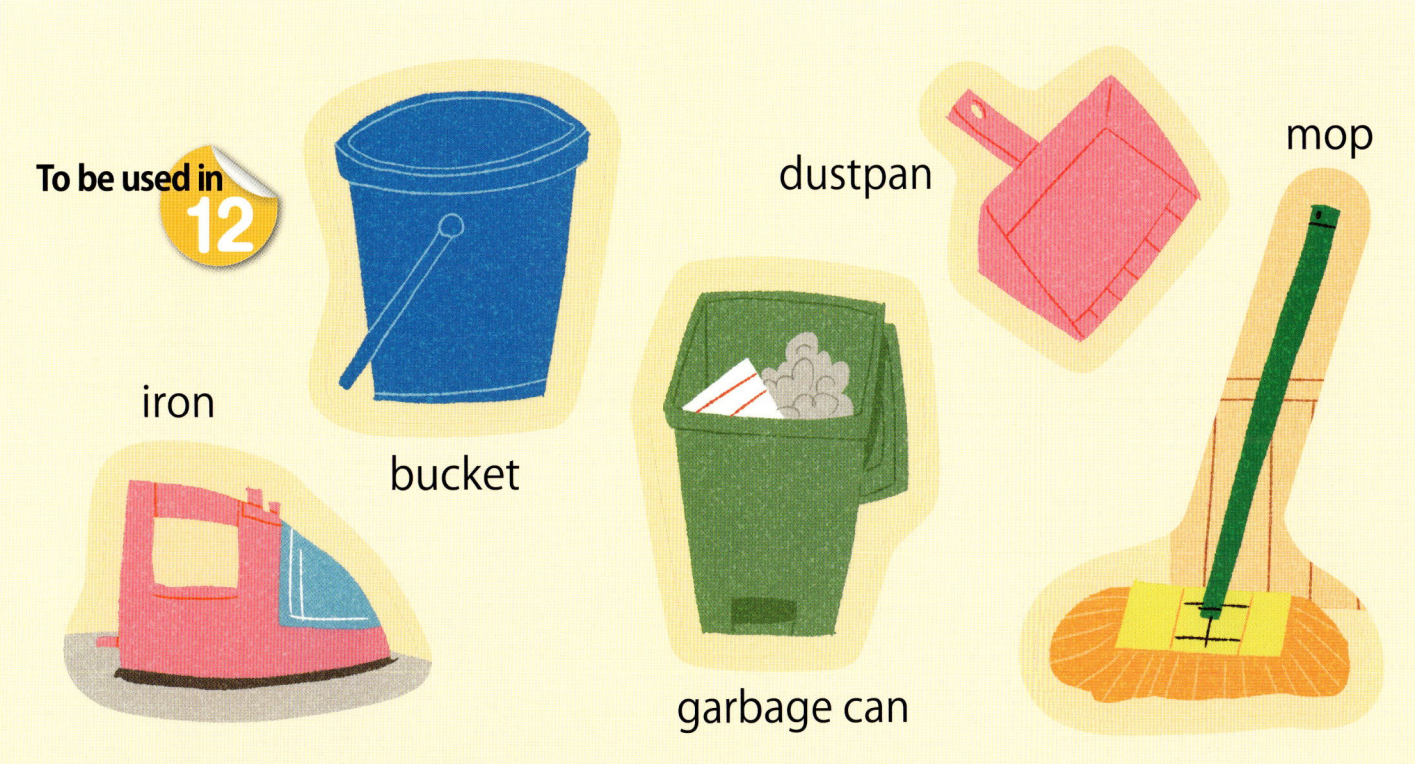

To be used in 13

night-light

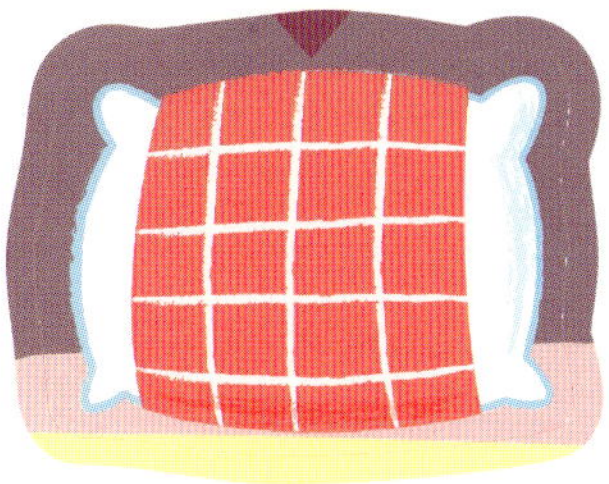

dresser

slippers

pillow

toy box

teddy bear

doll

pencil

To be used in 14

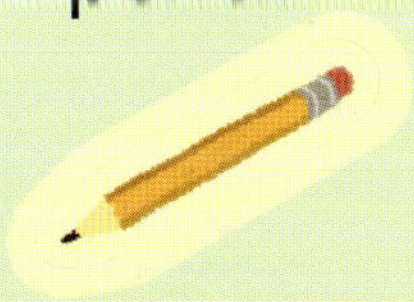

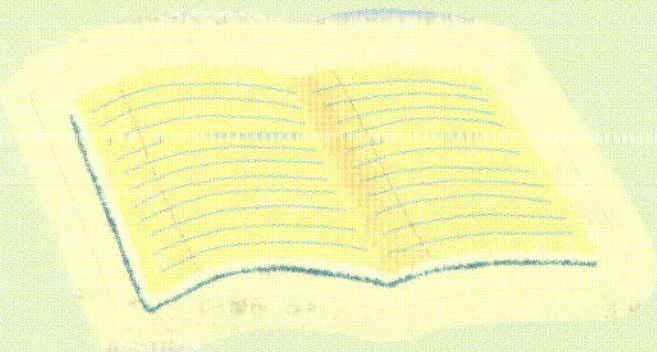

notebook

truck

book

ball

blocks

boat

cap

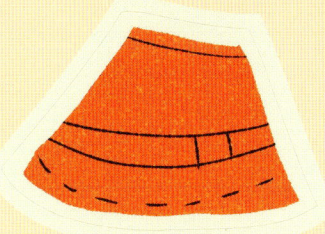

hat

shirt

sweater

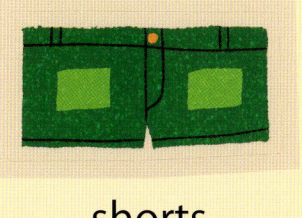

shorts

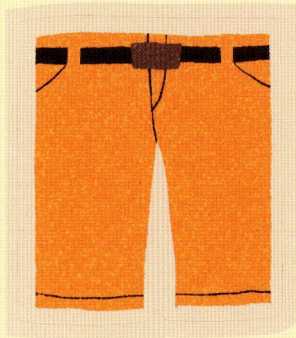

pants

boots

shoes